The PEACOCK AGENDA

by
Sean Pollock

Based on:
"The Peacock Agenda" (2018) by Marko Vignjevic

MONTAG

Montag Press ISBN: 978-1-940233-52-9
Design © 2020 Amit Dey

Montag Press Team:
Editor: Charlie Franco
Managing Director: Charlie Franco
Cover Image: Hannah Saeed

A Montag Press Book
www.montagpress.com
Montag Press
777 Morton Street, Unit B
San Francisco CA 94129 USA

Montag Press, the burning book with the hatchet cover, the skewed word mark and the portrayal of the long-suffering fireman mascot are trademarks of Montag Press.

Printed & Digitally Originated in the United States of America
10 9 8 7 6 5 4 3 2 1

But for the purposes of streaming or broadcasting, royalties are to be paid and cleared with Montag Press for all streaming rights including the following:

LIVE STREAMING - live performances streamed at specific show times.

SCHEDULED PERFORMANCE STREAMING - new productions captured 'on tape' and streamed at specific show times as scheduled content.

ON-DEMAND STREAMING - new productions captured 'on tape' and streamed for on-demand ticket sales at any time during a specific period of dates.

CHARACTERS
(3W, 5M)

WOMAN #1/DELIVERY WOMAN/COMMERCIAL VOICE/AIRPORT SECURITY/ENSEMBLE. 18-early 20's. A variety of characters, most prominent of which is Delivery Woman. Perhaps an ingenue type.

AYDA AYDUK: Mid 20's-30's. Our protagonist, a tortured young man trying to make sense of a barbaric world.

BALABAN: 60's-70's. Ayda's neighbor. Wise and fatherly.

PAVLE PECHULI/DELIVERY MAN/ENSEMBLE: Mid 20's-30's. An excitable young man and business owner, who shares Ayda's spirits for wanting something more/The delivery woman's replacement.

RADIO HOST/WAITRESS/WOMAN #2/FLIGHT ATTENDANT/ENSEMBLE. Late 20's-30's. A variety of characters, most prominent of which is the Flight Attendant. An everywoman.

DRAGA LAGRADA: 40's-50's. A giggly and warm, yet overbearing, mature woman of wealthy means. A glass half-full kind of woman, who counts her has over her has-nots. She knows that time is running out for her to find someone, so she is very accommodating. The love interest of Ayda.

ZAKORA/COSIMO LAGRADA/ENSEMBLE: 50's-70's. Ayda's boss, aggressive and rough around the edges/The pinnacle of wealth. Vice President of the Ethics Commission. Draga's father.

KROT/MEDIUM/ENSEMBLE: Early 20's. A young man who works in the morgue that Zakora slaps around/A medium Ayda meets on vacation.

A CASTING NOTE: Any actor of any race can play any role.

SETTING

An unspecified country.

TIME

The future.

PROLOGUE (AN EVENING ON THE WATER)

The stage is set as follows: Center stage is a shipping dock at the edge of town. Facing the audience, on one side of the dock, is a chain fence. Perhaps Christmas lights are strung over the top.

From the darkness, we see a silhouette of WOMAN #1. A glow of blue light surrounds her. She stares straight ahead in a very fixated manner--if she is in a trance. She blows a bright pink bubble out of bubblegum. Then she turns against the fence, back to the audience, with her arms outstretched like Christ. Suddenly, she dives off the platform to the water below, unseen to us.

Simultaneously, AYDA, an attractive young man, watches in a trench coat through a set of binoculars. Only the bow of the boat is represented here. He is looking arbitrarily into the distance. As the WOMAN dives, AYDA lowers the binoculars in disbelief. The corners of his mouth fold into a grim smile. A quick blackout.

SCENE TWO

The interior of AYDA's apartment. It is homely and comfortable.
A cross-stitch is hung on the wall along with a house phone with a
chord. Against the wall is a small stove where we hear the sizzling
of a pan. In front of the stove is a kitchen island. On top of the island
sits a small radio.

At the top of the scene, AYDA is at the island in an undershirt,
covered in blood. He is chopping up the torso of the woman from the
previous scene. He takes slabs of it and places it on a pan on the stove.
Something feel-good and retro is playing on the radio: something
like, "Get Happy" by Judy Garland or "A Summer Place" by Andy
Williams.

A few beats, and a knock at the door. AYDA stops what he's doing
and answers it. BALABAN, his neighbor, stands in the doorframe.
He wears a robe, slippers, a gold chain. He is holding a few letters.

BALABAN

Ayda, good to see you! *(acknowledges his shirt)* Oh my, you
have some--

AYDA

(acknowledging the shirt)

Yes, I'm aware. Balaban, how many times must I tell you
I wish you would wear something other than a robe
in my company.

BALABAN

Dear boy, I'm a creature of comfort, what can I say? *(beat)*
Well, are you going to invite me in?

AYDA

Well, I--

BALABAN

Smells good in here. Need a hand?

AYDA

I...I suppose.

BALABAN

So invite me in!

AYDA

(deadpan)
Balaban, won't you come in.

BALABAN

Thank you.

BALABAN enters the space, examines the torso on the table.

BALABAN

My my, it seems you caught a nice young woman by the looks
of it. A jumper?

AYDA

Indeed.

BALABAN

I'm guessing you found her late--after curfew?

AYDA

Sunday. No curfew.

BALABAN

Where was she jumping?

AYDA

The docks over by South Street.

BALABAN

The old Naval docks. God love 'em. You know I used to
gamble down there back in the day.

AYDA

So you've told me.

BALABAN

I haven't told you all of it, I know that much. Those were the days back then. Have a seat, my friend. Let me take over. You're exhausted, I can tell.

AYDA

I look that bad, huh?

BALABAN

Let me take care of the cooking, I insist.

AYDA

Someone's in a generous mood.

AYDA goes under the kitchen island, and produces two glasses and a bottle of wine. He pours the bottle of wine into the glasses. BALABAN begins taking over. BALABAN chops the body like loaves of bread, and takes it over to the stove to fry it.

BALABAN

Yeah, well, I suppose as of late, I've been trying to focus on nurturing the relationships I have while I'm still here.

AYDA

Oh, nonsense.

BALABAN

I supposed I needn't remind you my birthday is on Sunday?

AYDA

Oh, that's right--happy almost birthday.

BALABAN

Thank you. Five more years I get to stick around here, and I'm out. Then, I'm someone's lunch.

AYDA

I've been hearing that under special conditions, they're letting some of us live past 80 more and more if they can prove to the committees that they're still a contributing member of society. Especially since younger people are well...volunteering themselves to the committees in droves, like this one here.

BALABAN

Yes, well, I'm sure my daughter will say whatever she can to make sure I get the axe. She hates me.

AYDA

Well good riddance to her. You know you've always been like a father to me since I've lived here, Balaban.

BALABAN

And you, like the son I never had.

AYDA takes a wine glass and offers it to BALABAN.

AYDA

A toast.

BALABAN

A toast? To what?

AYDA

To chosen family.

BALABAN

To chosen family.

They clink and drink. Out of his robe pocket, BALABAN takes out some smokes.

BALABAN

Cigarette?

AYDA

Yes. Please.

BALABAN lights a cigarette. Hands one to AYDA. AYDA lights it.

BALABAN

Now, as your father figure, I must ask you: are there any
ladies in your life yet?

AYDA

This again.

BALABAN

You're too young to be so gloomy.

AYDA

Is that so?

BALABAN

You'll never attract a woman with all the inner darkness
practically radiating out of you, you know.

AYDA

Balaban, you know I don't socialize if I can avoid it. Plus we
live on this side of town where it stinks because of the mortuary. I couldn't be any more repellent to women if I tried.

BALABAN

Yes, but you're also fit and handsome. I mean, you have a
strapping frame.

AYDA

But what does it matter? I mean, half the time, I want to join
the jumpers and jump too.

BALABAN

If you want to join them, then what's stopping you?

AYDA

(after a moment:)
Sometimes, I really don't know.

BALABAN

Well, while you think about it--do you mind doing me a favor
and go downstairs and fetch my mail for me?

BALABAN takes a key out of his coat pocket and gives it to AYDA.

BALABAN

My knees hurt badly today. I simply can't be bothered to go
down the stairs.

AYDA

I'll be back.

BALABAN

I'll man the grill here.

Blackout.

SCENE THREE

*A mortuary. It is a dull dark room. A single light hangs above a slab.
On the wall is a magnetic knife holder with many knives hanging
on it, including a hacksaw and a cleaver. Also on the wall are some
Ethics Committee Propaganda posters, posters about sanitation laws,
a pin-up girl spread, a phone with a long chord, and a clock.*

*The island transforms into a slab. Next to the slab is an end table (or
a stool) with a radio on it. Something like "Boogie Woogie Bugle Boy"
by the Andrews Sisters faintly plays on the radio under the scene.*

*Lights dimly rise on ZAKORA, a large, tired looking man, reading the
paper eating a shoulder blade sandwich. Next to him is AYDA's breakfast: a hand on a bagel and eyeballs grilled in the style of hashbrowns.*

ZAKORA

(calling)
Krot! Krot!

Nothing.

ZAKORA

Ayda, have you seen Krot, and if not,
have you any idea why he isn't here?

AYDA

(offstage)
I haven't, Chief. Plus, we're out of coffee.

ZAKORA

Are you telling me that it's almost eight o'clock and there's no coffee?!

AYDA

No chief, there's nothing left to scrape.

ZAKORA

Jesus. Whose job was it to do inventory last?

AYDA enters in a work uniform with an empty coffee can.

AYDA

I believe it was yours, sir.

AYDA hands him the coffee pot. He begins to eat his sandwich.

AYDA

See? Nothing.

ZAKORA

So it's true: nothing will give us rise today! Where's that stupid boy? I'm going to send him for a coffee run.

AYDA

Technically, he's still early.

ZAKORA

Not early enough!

The sound of footsteps descending a staircase. Enter KROT, a disheveled young man in his worker's uniform.

KROT

Morning, Chief--and Ayda.

ZAKORA

Where in the rigor mortis were you, Krot!

KROT

Apologies sir.

ZAKORA

What happened? That girlfriend of yours wouldn't let you go this morning?

KROT

Something like that.

ZAKORA

You fucked last night?

KROT

Tore it up, I did.

ZAKORA

Kid, in every man's life a realization sets in, mostly too late, that it's quite the other way around.

KROT

The other way around, Chief?

ZAKORA

Yes. He realizes it was *he* who got fucked.

AYDA

I'm going to start getting the bodies ready.

AYDA exits.

KROT

But Chief, she did things to me.

ZAKORA

What things?

KROT

Well...down there.

ZAKORA

To a kid like you, an ideal blow job, is like pissing in the wind. So that's your excuse for being late? Some morning delight, I take it?

KROT

Kind of, sir.

ZAKORA

Kind of?

KROT

Yes. That's my excuse sir.

ZAKORA

Well, if it's hard and straight it's healthy. Just don't be late again.

ZAKORA takes out his wallet. AYDA re-enters with a Rubbermaid bin labeled "ARMS". He will later bring on more boxes that are obviously labeled with different labels such as "LEGS", "HANDS AND FINGERS", etc. AYDA stacks them by the door.

ZAKORA

In any event, we need coffee. Coffee is what we need. Another 30 oz. can, if you can. It's going to be a long day, we need to make sure it's spotless. The Morgue inspector is set to come at 12 to write a report so this place needs to be in top shape.

KROT

Yes, sir.

AYDA re-enters with another box. KROT begins to leave.

KROT

Oh um...Ayda? I hate to ask this--but are you going
to finish that hand sandwich? I didn't have time to have
breakfast. I'll get you back at the end of the day, I just don't
want to waste anymore time.

AYDA

All yours.

*AYDA hands him the sandwich and exits. KROT begins to leave.
ZAKORA goes back to reading the paper.*

KROT

You think she'll be on time this time? She was late yesterday.

ZAKORA

You're obsessed, you pervert.

KROT

Try and stall her. I don't want to miss her.

ZAKORA

Every day you come in here describing your sex love at home
with a woman who might as well be a succubus who won't let
you out of her clutches, and you're bent out of shape trying
to make sure you don't miss the delivery girl?

KROT

You've a wife, and I've seen the way you look at her too,
chief!

ZAKORA

Oh, be gone with you, boy!

KROT

Make sure the delivery girl doesn't leave before
I get here!

ZAKORA

Get coffee, you idiot!

KROT exits. AYDA re-enters with a bin.

ZAKORA

You're such a pushover, Ayda. Letting that half-wit take your
breakfast on top of being late. It's like assault and battery.

AYDA

The hand was quite undercooked anyway. The scrambled
eyeballs on the other hand aren't bad.

ZAKORA

The hands are always hit or miss there I find. *(beat)* You
know that reminds me, I actually have some left over hand

chowder downstairs that I could really go for right now, I'm going to go get that. Come with me and go get the bins.

They both exit. A knock at the door. A moment. Another knock. AYDA re-enters with a bin, and answers the door. Enter the DELIVERY WOMAN.

DELIVERY WOMAN

Morning.

AYDA

Morning.

DELIVERY WOMAN

How many bins have we today?

AYDA

Just one more in the back.

DELIVERY WOMAN

Do you want me to go with?

AYDA

No, I--

DELIVERY WOMAN

Sorry. I meant. Do you need help?

AYDA

I got it, I think.

AYDA exits. A moment. ZAKORA re-enters.

ZAKORA

Oh! Didn't know you were here.

DELIVERY WOMAN

Morning, chief.

ZAKORA

And how are we today?

DELIVERY WOMAN

Same old.

ZAKORA

Ah.

ZAKORA goes to read the paper. He keeps sneaking glances at her. She looks away.

ZAKORA

You look different today.

DELIVERY WOMAN

Is that so?

ZAKORA

A haircut, maybe?

DELIVERY WOMAN

No.

ZAKORA

Perhaps a...recoloring?

DELIVERY WOMAN

No.

ZAKORA studies her.

ZAKORA

Perhaps it's your arms. They seem to have more...tone.

DELIVERY WOMAN

Oh...um. Thank you.

ZAKORA

Most men are threatened when a woman has
muscles, but...not me.

DELIVERY WOMAN

Good to know.

ZAKORA

Mm.

Re-enter AYDA with a bin.

AYDA

This is the last one.

DELIVERY WOMAN

Okay. *(beat)* It's always so nice that you label them for me.

AYDA

What do you mean?

DELIVERY WOMAN

The bins. When I drop them off at the factory, they always make me go through all of my deliveries and make me label them in arrangements by parts before they're distributed. It saves me a lot of time.

AYDA

Oh.

DELIVERY WOMAN

Yeah.

AYDA

I wasn't aware of that.

She smiles at AYDA, warmly.

AYDA

So, uh...should we load these into the truck?

DELIVERY WOMAN

Sure.

DELIVERY WOMAN takes one end of the bin, and AYDA the other. They exit. Blackout.

SCENE FOUR

Back at the dock again. This scene mirrors the setup of that in the Prologue--on one part of the stage is AYDA watching in a trench coat and binoculars. Only the bow of the boat is represented here.

The sound of rain.

From the darkness, we see a silhouette of a MAN in a suit, drinking a bottle of something in a bag. He is stumbling. He is hysterical. He erupts in laughter, but then starts to cry.

MAN

What's the point! What's the point in all of this!

The MAN begins taking off his clothes.

MAN

Free me from these earthly possessions! I'm free! I'm free! I'm--

The MAN suddenly stumbles backwards and falls off the dock. The sound of his body hitting the water. The lights strike an oceanic blue.

MAN

(calling out)
Help me! Help me!

AYDA looks alert and paddles towards him.

The sounds of rain and the waves reverberate as we go into the next scene:

SCENE FIVE

Back at AYDA's apartment. AYDA is brewing a pot of tea. A glass of water is placed on the kitchen island. After a few moments, enter the MAN from earlier.

MAN

Where am I?

AYDA

Oh, hello. I was wondering when you'd be up.

MAN

Who are you?

AYDA

Ayda Ayduk.

A silence.

MAN

I feel awful.

AYDA

I would imagine so.

MAN

What happened? Where did you find me?

AYDA

You fell into the water by the docks.

MAN

(piecing it together)
And I...I took off all my clothes, and that's why I don't have any.

MAN presses his temples.

MAN

My head.

AYDA

Here.

AYDA goes under the kitchen island, takes out a bottle of painkillers and gives it to the MAN, along with a glass of water. MAN takes the pills and throws back the water.

MAN

So I fell into the water, hm?

AYDA

Yes.

MAN

And you saved me?

AYDA

I suppose.

MAN

I was so far gone. I really could've died.

AYDA

You're lucky it's summer. A winter's death is ten times more uncomfortable.

MAN

Did I...did I jump?

AYDA

I couldn't quite tell.

MAN

Now that I'm thinking about it...I know I wanted to jump. I had really lost my mind back there. *(beat)* What were you doing there anyway, in the water? Especially after curfew--you could've been thrown in jail for being out there that late on a weeknight. We both could've!

AYDA

Well, if you must know I often come so I can...go after those who jump.

MAN

And why is that?

AYDA

It feels better to me, in the world that we live in today, to only feast on the flesh of those who offer themselves willingly.

MAN

As opposed to the ones who are--?

AYDA

Yes. Those people often don't want to die--they are just sentenced to.

MAN

What are we gonna do? Protest? They'll gas us again.

AYDA

If we are to live in this...this barbaric society where we must eat each other, I'd really rather only eat upon those who give themselves to the cause. Truthfully, I avoid eating out whenever I can. I still can never just get used to this way of living.

MAN

I wish there were still plants and animals to eat. *(after a moment)* Anyway, this all feels so...curious. Truthfully, I feel embarrassed. My drunken antics have led me into quite the predicament here. I barely have clothes and I'm in a stranger's house...*(beat)* Say, you didn't do anything funny to me while I was asleep, right?

AYDA

Ha! I wouldn't dream of it.

MAN

What is your name anyway, kind stranger?

AYDA

Ayda. And you?

MAN

Pavle. Pavle Pechuli.

They shake hands.

AYDA

How do you do?

PAVLE

(laughing)
How do you do indeed?

AYDA

Pechuli. That name sounds familiar to me.

PAVLE

I own a business downtown called Pechuli's Den you may
have heard of.

AYDA

Ah--yes. Right near the Jewelry District.

PAVLE

That's the one!

AYDA

What kind of business is taxidermy nowadays?

PAVLE

An infrequent one.

AYDA

I could see that.

PAVLE

On that note, I suppose I should...go and shower off. I have river reek all over me. Not to trouble you more than I already have, but, do you have any clothes I can borrow? I will, of course, give them back.

AYDA

I believe I do--I'll go fetch some.

PAVLE

Thank you, again. Sincerely--I don't know how I can repay you.

AYDA

How's about we sit down sometime and you can get me a tea and perhaps attempt to explain your drunken antics, so to speak.

PAVLE

That can certainly be arranged. Which way is the restroom?

AYDA

Down the hall. There's fresh linens in the closet.

PAVLE begins to walk away.

AYDA

After you leave my care, you're not going to try and jump
again are you?

PAVLE

Certainly not. I have a shop to run in the morning.

The kettle whistles. AYDA turns down the stove.

PAVLE

This...this all feels so terribly awkward and embarrassing. I
really can't thank you enough.

AYDA smiles. He begins preparing the tea.

SCENE SIX

Pavle's shop. PAVLE is dusting the counter. The shop is decorated with taxidermied animals, clocks, wigheads, a small chest full of old photographs and other knick-knacks. A radio sits on the counter.

RADIO HOST (O.S)

And a reminder folks to wash your hands, say hello to your neighbor, and most importantly, make every day a brighter one for someone else. This message is brought to you by the Ethics Committee. And now, for a musical break.

Something like "Tammy" by Debbie Reynolds plays. Enter DRAGA LAGRADA, dressed lavishly in sunglasses and a posh jacket with a peacock feather pinned to it with two breast pockets. As she enters, the bell chimes.

PAVLE

Afternoon, Ms. Lagrada.

DRAGA

Pavle, how are you dear?

PAVLE

I'm well, my dear. I'm assuming you're here for the bird.

DRAGA

Yes, yes, darling.

PAVLE

I'll go and get it.

DRAGA

Mind if I change the station?

PAVLE

Go for it.

DRAGA changes the radio station. She changes it to something like "Ain't Misbehavin'" by Fats Waller. PAVLE re-enters with a giant, heavy, turquoise and sea-blue-colored taxidermied peacock with fantastical feathers.

PAVLE

Here we are Ms. Draga.

DRAGA

Pavle, it's magnificent. Why it's the most peculiar--but beautiful--creature I've ever seen.

PAVLE

It wasn't easy to find one quite like this. This is a once-in-a-lifetime peacock.

DRAGA

I'm positively reeling! Magnifique!! J'adore!! It's going to be so hard to hide this for 10 whole months! Papa is going to be absolutely weak. No one will be able to top a gift like this for his 70th! Where ever did you find...?

PAVLE

Estate sale in Essex. Every now and then, something wonderful turns up. It's got to be at least 70, maybe even 80 years old.

DRAGA

Have you a gift box?

PAVLE

As a matter of fact, I do. But I hardly think that'll make it look less conspicuous if you're trying to hide it.

DRAGA

A suitcase? I will obviously return it.

PAVLE

Let me check.

PAVLE exits. AYDA enters. The bell chimes. DRAGA turns around from the peacock and her interest suddenly piques.

DRAGA

Hello.

AYDA

Oh, hello. Is um...Pavle here?

DRAGA

As a matter of fact he is. But he's out back at the moment...
maybe there's something I could help you with?

AYDA

Do you...work here?

DRAGA

No. But I drop by often. I know this place like the back of
my hand.

AYDA

Oh. Well I'm just here to pay him a visit.

DRAGA

Are you two friends?

AYDA

Acquaintances, I would say.

Re enter Pechuli with a suitcase covered in stickers

PAVLE

Oh, Ayda! You came! Draga La--

DRAGA

I'm Draga. Pleasure to meet you, Mr. Ayda.

AYDA

I've come to receive thanks.

PAVLE

You made the time. I'm glad to see. Right now I'm just
finishing up Ms. La--

DRAGA

Pavle. Please, how many times must I tell you to just call me
Draga.

PAVLE

Right. Well, Ms. Draga this thing is rather heavy and I doubt
you will be able to carry it yourself all the way home.

DRAGA

Oh, nonsense. Let me just put the bird into the suitcase.

DRAGA attempts to put the bird in the suitcase and really obviously struggles. It is awkward and drawn out.

AYDA

Miss--? I think I can help.

AYDA pulls up his shirt sleeves and lifts the suitcase.

DRAGA

Oh, what a gentleman!

PAVLE

Stop by again, Ayda! I'll see you in a while and get you that drink you promised.

AYDA

Farewell!

DRAGA opens the door for AYDA. They leave the store.

DRAGA

I'm just up the way some. Thank you ever so much for helping me.

AYDA

(clearly struggling)
My pleasure.

DRAGA

Such a gentleman of you to help me with my bird. I know it's heavy, but you are handling it quite well.

AYDA

It's not so bad.

DRAGA

So Mr. Ayda, are you from around these parts?

AYDA

Indeed. I live in Yardley Circus.

DRAGA

Raised there as well?

AYDA

Been in the same apartment for over 25 years, if you can
believe it.

DRAGA

Do you live with your family still?

AYDA

No, no. My father passed a few years back.

DRAGA

And your mother?

AYDA

I never knew her. She left after I was born.

DRAGA

I'm sorry to hear that.

AYDA

And you?

DRAGA

Also born and raised here. As embarrassed as I am to admit it, I still live with my parents, but the truth is their place really is stunning. I'd be downgrading if I lived anywhere else. In fact, we're approaching it right now.

AYDA

(pointing in the distance)
Is this it?

DRAGA

Mhm. Here, hand it to me--I can take it from here.

AYDA hands her the bird, and she drops it almost immediately. They laugh. AYDA picks it up, and hands it to her. He doesn't quite remove the bird from his arms and their arms become interlocked.

DRAGA

The elevator's out once again--I couldn't possibly ask you to walk all the way up. Here, I'll take it.

AYDA

How about we both carry it?

DRAGA smiles.

DRAGA

Well, alright...

AYDA

And you know...um...can I ask, what are you doing this weekend?

DRAGA

I don't know off the top of my head...why?

AYDA

Would you like to have dinner with me tomorrow evening?

DRAGA

That would be really lovely. But can we get this peacock upstairs first?

AYDA

Of course.

They laugh, and walk offstage with the peacock in arms.

SCENE SEVEN

The scene bleeds seamlessly into an upscale restaurant. DRAGA and AYDA sit at a table with a basket of rolls placed onto it along with a small jar of guts. A candle is lit. Something like the 1976 cast album of "Carmen" faintly plays in the background.

DRAGA

So do you...come here often?

AYDA

On occasion. I like the food here.

DRAGA

You look like you don't go out much.

AYDA

Was I clumsy when I asked you out?

DRAGA

We were holding a giant bird that weighed 100 pounds, so I'd say perhaps a little.

They share a laugh.

DRAGA

When you asked, it was if you were saying something you already knew.

AYDA

I wasn't saying anything I already knew. I was expressing hope.

DRAGA

Hope?

AYDA

Hope that if I were clumsy that it was funny or endearing in some way, perhaps?

DRAGA

It was both, to tell you the truth.

AYDA

The truth will set you free, right?

DRAGA

The truth won't set you free but the truth will oblige you.

Enter a WAITRESS. She is dressed very conservatively. Her uniform is reminiscent of a 1920's maid.

WAITRESS

Good evening sir and madame. How are we this evening?

DRAGA

Just lovely, and you, dear?

WAITRESS

Just splendid. Would you like me to read off for you the specials for today?

DRAGA

Sure, go ahead.

WAITRESS

So today we have terrific eye socket noodles with gallbladder ragu that has a bit of a spicier blend; which pairs nicely with our house ale. We also have a skin flake salad with fried eyeballs and a syrupy blood glaze; which pairs pleasantly with a sauvignon blanc. We also have roasted forearm this evening which is baked in our fire brick stove completed with steamed intenses on the side; which pairs splendidly with cabernet sauvignon.

DRAGA

Ooh, I should love the roasted forearm and steamed intestines. You said it came with what kind of wine again?

WAITRESS

The cabernet sauvignon.

DRAGA

You know, I think I'll swap it out for a Vieux Carre.

WAITRESS

An excellent choice, madame. The lemon clone selection we have here is fantastic. *(to Ayda)* And for you?

AYDA

I think I'll do the same.

WAITRESS

Wonderful. We'll be out with that soon.

WAITRESS takes their menu and exits. A moment. DRAGA smiles at him.

AYDA

What are you smiling about?

DRAGA

Is there a reason I shouldn't be smiling?

AYDA

No, no I just--I was wondering if maybe you were thinking of something that made you laugh, or something.

DRAGA

I suppose there was one thing.

AYDA

And what is that?

DRAGA

I was thinking about how I hadn't been here in many years on a date and at this point in my life, I had sort of accepted that that was probably the last time I'd come here on a date and now, here I am. I was just reminiscing is all. *(beat)* Would you mind if I had nibbled on some of a roll?

AYDA

Of course, not. That's what they're there for.

DRAGA

I know but. I...well, you know. It's improper for a woman to take the first one. I think I should fancy a bit of guts on mine. Would you want any?

AYDA

I'm fine, thank you.

DRAGA takes a bite off the roll, and polishes it with some guts.

AYDA

So um, who were you on the date with?

DRAGA

Oh, surely you don't want to know that. It's not polite to talk
about exes, especially the first time out.

AYDA

Was he an ex, or someone you went on a date with? There is
a difference, my sweet.

DRAGA

Just a date. He was a captain, actually.

AYDA

A captain?

DRAGA

Yes. The captain of a port ship. We were young. I think
I might have even been twenty-five, if you could believe it.
I'm telling you, it was a long time ago. I remember he was
very handsome. He had blue eyes and dark brown eyes. He
had such a husky, deep voice. But, I think we maybe stopped
seeing each other because his schedule was busy, or perhaps
he lost interest in me and didn't have the heart to tell me.
I'm not sure.

AYDA

Ah. I'm sorry.

DRAGA

Don't be. If it had worked out, I wouldn't be here tonight, would I? It's important to remain in the present. Anyway, it's no matter now. *(beat)* So tell me. What is it like working in the morgues here?

AYDA

It's pretty boring. Nothing about my job is something you should want to discuss over dinner.

DRAGA

Well dinner's not here yet!

AYDA

It wouldn't be proper.

DRAGA

Oh, who cares about proper! Proper shmopper.

AYDA

All that's worth mentioning is that I spend a lot of time dissecting and dismembering the dead. It becomes very routine. I've built a great tolerance to the smell of decomposition and not a whole lot tends to phase me. It is sort of business as usual. In the same way as Mr. Pechuli has developed a routine for taxidermy, I'm sure.

DRAGA

I suppose so. Up until this moment, I hadn't put much thought into it.

Enter the WAITRESS with food on a serving tray.

AYDA

Perhaps we should talk about something else--as I suggested earlier this is hardly good dinner conversation, it's so dreary, really.

DRAGA

(acknowledging the WAITRESS)
Speaking of...

WAITRESS

Alright, two Vieux Carres and two orders of the roasted forearm and seasoned intestines.

WAITRESS serves DRAGA and AYDA their meals.

WAITRESS

Is there anything else I can get for either of you?

DRAGA

I believe we're set for now, thank you.

WAITRESS

My pleasure. Feel free to call me over should you need.

WAITRESS exits.

AYDA

Well...cheers.

DRAGA

Cheers!

They clink glasses. Both take a sip and then begin eating. After a moment or so:

AYDA

What do you think?

DRAGA takes a sip of her drink.

AYDA

The question was put to you too soon. I see that now. That's why I'll continue talking until you finish with that bite. Personally, I always thought well of people who harbor a good, healthy appetite. Perhaps it's a sign they don't feel embarrassed about their wants, their current needs, be they as simple and everyday as food needs. As you can see, I also eat a bit fast. I have no tolerance for the lack of freshness when it comes to food. *(beat)* So it appears you agree. I'll take that to mean that you're happy with your meal, both because it was your choice and because it's fresh food. Good, I'd hate to have that waiter explain themself and the manner of the proprietor's cuisine choices.

DRAGA laughs and covers her mouth with the napkin.

AYDA

I can continue on if you'd like.

DRAGA

I think it's wonderful. Take it in, darling. I should hope we have similar tastes.

AYDA

If you insist.

AYDA begins to eat.

DRAGA

Ayda, I should like to tell you now that you needn't worry about the check here.

AYDA

And why is that? Surely you're not going to tell me you're going to pay!

DRAGA

I appreciate the chivalry, really—and I wouldn't want to come across as patronizing—but with a salary as small as yours (I'd imagine), I'd feel impolite putting the strain on you. The reason I bring it up is because well, for most places in town, I'm not charged because of my father. While perhaps I should've held off this conversation for a later time, I'd rather get it out of the way now because I enjoy your company. You know who my father is, right?

AYDA

No, I can't say that I do. Is it someone I should know?

DRAGA

I'm sure Pavle told you. There's no need to be coy.

AYDA

No, really, he didn't say a word. I hadn't even told him we were going out. We only really met once.

DRAGA

How do you two know each other again?

AYDA

(briskly changing the subject)
Finish what you were saying though—your father is who, now?

DRAGA

Does the name Cosimo Lagrada ring a bell to you?

AYDA

I've seen that name in papers before, but I can't recall off the top of my head.

DRAGA

He's the Vice President of the Ethics Committee.

AYDA

(surprised)
Oh.

DRAGA

I know it's...well. Let's just say his position has helped me in all but affairs of romantic nature.

A moment. AYDA thinks on this and continues eating.

DRAGA

I know to some it may seem like I live a sheltered life--but I've always managed to keep an ear to the ground. I know that my father is the most disliked person in the country next to the President of the Committee himself, Sir Aksoy--

AYDA

My dear, all I care about is this meal with you now. It doesn't bother me who your father is or isn't. We don't choose our families in this life.

DRAGA

That's incredibly sweet of you, Ayda. You are such a gentleman.

AYDA

Nonsense. We can talk more on the subject later if you wish, but you shouldn't worry what I think of your family. We're just starting to get to know each other, and after all, I am on a date with you--not your father.

She laughs. They continue eating.

DRAGA

You know, after this I should fancy a bon-bon.

AYDA

Well...I would be worried about adding more to the bill.

DRAGA

Oh, you devil, you!

They laugh.

SCENE EIGHT

Back at the morgue. The corpse of a man sits on the slab, covered by a white sheet. ZAKORA and KROT are observing it, lifting the sheet up to their faces. ZAKORA holds a flashlight. KROT wears a surgical mask. On the end of the slab is a bucket, which KROT scoops the organs into.

ZAKORA

What do you think?

KROT

It looks sort of familiar to me.

ZAKORA

I was thinking the same thing. The skull is very bumpy. Bulbus, even.

KROT

Even his irregular bones are regular.

ZAKORA

You know what? I think this was the man over in Eastminster where I grew up who used to be a florist. I always did wonder what happened to him once there were no more flowers.

KROT

I've read of flowers, but never seen one myself.

ZAKORA

I was young but they were nice.

Enter AYDA in his work uniform with some labeled boxes from earlier.

ZAKORA

Ayda, take a look at this man. Does he look familiar to you?

AYDA crosses to them, observing the corpse. KROT continues to scoop out the guts.

AYDA

No.

ZAKORA

Look at the body though. How do you suppose he died? It looks like a natural death to me.

A silence from AYDA.

ZAKORA

Now would be a good time to add your thoughts.

AYDA

What?

ZAKORA

Do you find natural death interesting?

AYDA

I don't know.

ZAKORA

What are you, some sort of nut who works toward a state of grave activity? By rigor mortis, man, don't work only for the grave.

AYDA

I agree, Chief, my mind just wandered away for a minute. Do you find him dull as well?

ZAKORA

As dull as an old man's after lunch nap.

AYDA

I'm going to get the rest of the bins.

KROT

When is the delivery girl coming?

ZAKORA

Ten, as always!

KROT

What is the time anyway?

ZAKORA consults his watch.

ZAKORA

Fifteen to.

KROT yawns.

ZAKORA

Didn't you get enough sleep last night,
or is it too soon to ask?

KROT

I was with my girlfriend last night.

ZAKORA

Oh really? Your girlfriend now?

KROT

I was throbbing for a bobbing, Chief, I had no choice.

ZAKORA

Krot, you really are a horny little corpse to be.

KROT

What isn't crazy has no psyche, Chief.

ZAKORA

But it does need rest.

AYDA re-enters, bringing on another box, exits.

ZAKORA

Is she hotter than the delivery girl?

KROT

I think so.

ZAKORA

You *think* so, or you know so?

KROT

The delivery girl has bigger breasts, but my girl has a bigger ass. It's a matter of preference.

KROT crosses to the magnetic knife holder and takes out a magnetic hack saw. He hands a knife to ZAKORA. They begin to chop up the body. We hear the sound of the hacksaw grounding the bone.

ZAKORA

I really think it's all about the face. Neither are much good without a pleasing face.

KROT

I've heard it say ugly women put out better because they feel the need to overcompensate, and I can certainly say that has proven true in my days at school. I bumped uglies with some real beasts.

ZAKORA

You dog.

KROT

I suppose my girlfriend is more attractive than the delivery girl to me because she has a fuller figure, which is something I always find attractive. The delivery girl has a more traditional kind of beauty.

ZAKORA

Was she pure before she met you?

KROT

She said she was, but a girl with a mouth as talented as hers--I wouldn't be surprised if she was lying to appease me.

ZAKORA

I wonder if the delivery girl is a virgin or not.

KROT

Surely not.

ZAKORA

She must have an idea of how gorgeous she is. She can afford to save herself. I haven't noticed a ring on her finger.

KROT

If she were married, it wouldn't be wise to wear a ring to work. It could get dirty or lost.

ZAKORA

But if she were married, what kind of husband would let his wife work as a delivery girl for morgues? It's a disgusting job. No job for a wife. Besides, he'd be letting her just roam about horny pigs such as the likes of us all day.

KROT

Perhaps he's more open-minded. Your wife works with men, does she not? Does that mean they all want to get in bed with her?

ZAKORA

She works for the Chamber of Commerce with a
bunch of mopey pencil-pushers. I'm no fruit, but I can tell
you enough to tell you that none of them would be
worth cheating on me for.

*The DELIVERY WOMAN enters. A knock at the door. Almost
synchronistically, AYDA enters on with the last box, a clipboard
with an inventory list on it and a pen.*

AYDA

I'll get it. It's probably her.

ZAKORA

She's early.

*AYDA opens the door and the DELIVERY WOMAN enters the
space.*

AYDA

Hello.

DELIVERY WOMAN

Hi. How are you today?

AYDA

I'm well. Everything's loaded up.

DELIVERY WOMAN

Great.

AYDA

A bit lighter than usual.

DELIVERY WOMAN

Less for me to carry then.

ZAKORA

Morning.

DELIVERY WOMAN

(acknowledging him and KROT)
Hi.

DELIVERY WOMAN crosses to the boxes. She takes two and exits.

ZAKORA

Look at her. Two boxes at a time. She is strong.

KROT

So it would appear.

ZAKORA

God I would do anything for an excuse to get closer to that chest of hers.

KROT

Maybe you could hand a box off to her and pretend to drop it and grab onto one.

ZAKORA

The thought had occurred to me.

DELIVERY WOMAN re-enters and takes another box. Exits. A silence. AYDA turns on the radio. Something like "I'm Falling In Love With Someone" or "Lover Come Back To Me" by Nelson Eddy plays.

ZAKORA

Be careful with that thing. You're not cutting that right.

KROT

I'm trying.

ZAKORA

Boy, you're going to get nowhere cutting it like that. Let me to it—I've the cleaver. It's much easier to cut it with a cleaver.

ZAKORA takes the cleaver. A loud chop.

ZAKORA

It's much easier that way.

KROT

Ah.

AYDA

Finished with the inventory list.

DELIVERY WOMAN re-enters.

AYDA

Oh, here. I'll just take this one for you.

DELIVERY WOMAN

Are you sure?

AYDA

I've a moment.

DELIVERY WOMAN

My truck is right out there.

AYDA puts the pen behind his ear and takes the last box and exits with the DELIVERY WOMAN.

KROT

Lucky bastard.

ZAKORA

If he's not back in five minutes, I'll call him in, that swine.

KROT

He's got the same idea we do.

ZAKORA

(sarcastically)
You think?

A moment.

ZAKORA

This is coming along rather nicely.

The lights shift to outside the morgue. DELIVERY WOMAN and AYDA re-enter.

DELIVERY WOMAN

Thanks for taking that out.

AYDA

No problem.

DELIVERY WOMAN

Do you mind if I borrow your pen for a moment?

AYDA

Sure.

He lends her his pen. She takes out a piece of paper from her pocket. She scribbles something down. She hands the piece of paper to him.

DELIVERY WOMAN

Here's my number if you need anything. My name is Irina.

AYDA

Oh, um. Thank you. I'm not sure why I would need this, but I appreciate it.

IRINA

I just thought maybe...*(beat)* I don't know. I'll see you around.

IRINA exits. Blackout.

The lighting shifts and we are at the docks. Classical music plays, something like Bach. AYDA is in his boat. The setup from the Prologue is mirrored--but with WOMAN #2.

WOMAN #2 is very nervous and shaking. Her makeup runs down her face. She has shackles around her wrists and is holding an anchor. She jumps.

AYDA paddles to rescue her.

SCENE NINE

AYDA's apartment. Seated is PAVLE, next to an end table, smoking a cigarette and drinking an Irish coffee. On the end table is another Irish coffee and an ashtray. On the island is a glass of water and a radio.

PAVLE

So you have seen her since?

AYDA

(offstage)
Yes, in fact, we've been out a few times.

PAVLE

It sounds like things are improving. Before you know it, you'll even have real regrets. *(beat)* Do you want to hear a joke?

AYDA

(offstage)
Can it wait for a moment?

PAVLE

What does an architect call his dog's house?

A silence.

PAVLE

I said, what does an architect call his dog's house? *(beat)*
A Bauchaus!

He laughs at his own joke. A silence.

PAVLE

Ok, I'll try another one. So, two bullets go off and meet
each other mid-air.
What do they say to each other?

A silence.

PAVLE

Oh dammit, they fired you too?!

*He laughs. AYDA re-enters with a cigar box, changed from his work
outfit.*

AYDA

How's the coffee?

PAVLE

Fantastic. Perfect amount of whiskey. Yours is going to get
cold soon. *(acknowledging the box)*
What's in that?

AYDA

Here. I haven't touched them in a while, but I figured the occasion called for it.

Hands PAVLE the cigar box. PAVLE opens it.

PAVLE

Are these...?

AYDA

Cigars. They were my father's.

PAVLE

Heavens! You could make a small fortune from these!

AYDA

Some things are better left off the market, I think.

PAVLE

How did *he* get them?

AYDA

They've been in my family for generations now.

PAVLE

How did they survive the war?

AYDA

I don't know, but, here they are. They are fine though, in
nearly perfect condition. I should think one between us will
be more than enough.

PAVLE

I'm honored you'd consider to share at all.

*From the cigar box, AYDA takes a zippo and ensures to turn the end
of the cigar close to the flame and rotates the cigar to make sure the
end is evenly light. He coughs.*

PAVLE

Oh my.

AYDA

It has been a while.

*AYDA continues to cough. He crosses to the counter and gets the glass
of water.*

PAVLE

You sure you're going to be ok over there?

AYDA

Would you still want to try?

PAVLE

Certainly!

AYDA hands the cigar to PAVLE, who inhales without so much of a clearing of the throat.

AYDA

How do you refrain from coughing?

PAVLE

You just take a little at a time. Don't inhale quite as much.

AYDA

Would you like me to put the radio on?

PAVLE

Sure.

AYDA, still coughing, turns the radio on. Something like "Take Five" by Dave Brubeck plays.

PAVLE

Really, thank you for sharing this with me. It's quite kind of you.

AYDA

I don't have company much, so I figured I'd break one out, for a special occasion.

PAVLE

I'll take it as a thank you for introducing you to
Ms. Lagrada then?

AYDA

If you intend to take it as such, so it shall be.

PAVLE

And, speak of the devil...

AYDA

I knew this was going to come.

PAVLE

You can't blame me for being curious.

AYDA

It's...it's going fine, thank you.

PAVLE

Did you really not recognize her that day of the shop? Did
you really not know who her father was?

AYDA

I'd no idea he was Vice President of the Ethics Committee
until she brought it up. How would I know what he looks
like anyway?

PAVLE

Can I ask you something a bit personal?

AYDA

You can ask whatever you please, but depending on what it is, I may or may not answer it.

PAVLE

Why an older woman?

A silence.

AYDA

I don't know, really. I hadn't put much thought in it. She seemed nice, I suppose.

PAVLE

Nice?

AYDA

I guess I didn't think of it right away.

PAVLE

I find it's often the time that men like us are expected to find younger women more attractive, but I personally I agree with you--I find a curvacious, more mature woman with large breasts just as erotic. *(beat)* You'd ever consider sharing her with another man?

A moment. PAVLE looks into AYDA's eyes and inhales the cigar. Then he laughs, hard. AYDA laughs along, nervously. PAVLE briefly grabs AYDA's thigh, then goes to sip his coffee.

PAVLE

Surely you've told her now the truth of how we met by now.

AYDA

(hesitantly)
...No.

PAVLE

Do you intend to?

AYDA

Not until it's...it's gotten serious.

PAVLE

Does it feel serious, or does it feel casual? How many times have you been out now?

AYDA

Two...three times now.

PAVLE

Does she know you go out to the docks for jumpers?

AYDA

No.

PAVLE

When *was* the last time you went out there?

AYDA

Last week.

PAVLE

What kind is it that you have now?

AYDA

What kind?

PAVLE

What type is maybe a better way of asking.

AYDA

I don't know what you mean.

PAVLE

Let's start this way. Is your meal this week a man or a woman?

AYDA

Does it matter?

PAVLE

I'm just interested, is all. Does it really feel easier once you put a face to what's on your plate?

AYDA

If you don't understand why I do what I do, that is fine, in the same way that I don't try to poke and prod about why you jumped.

PAVLE

You know why I jumped? Because this whole world is a madhouse, and who would know better than I? I spend my hard earned coin going to estate sales and reading history books, and buying off artifacts. I wish so badly that we existed in the kind of life before the war. I feel so close to it in so many ways. We're just living to die and you know it, man. There is more to this life than working, eating bread and flesh and having curfews on work nights or we'll be thrown in jail by the Ethics Patrol--there has to be. And it disgusts you too, that's why you can't even dine on the meat of those whose hands you run through every day. You've seen them mutated in the worst of ways. You know too much.

AYDA

In more ways than one, I'm inclined to agree with that assessment.

PAVLE

I should say, I don't think less of you for dining on the jumpers. It makes sense to me. I'm just asking for the sake of
conversation.

AYDA

You know, I suppose the only reason I haven't jumped myself
is because I think there might still be a way out of all of this.
Maybe one day, I'll be able to work in another country or
something if I work hard enough and it'll be better and get
to do something else.

PAVLE

Your optimism fascinates me. You know it's virtually impos-
sible to get permission to even leave the country for more
than thirty days.*(beat)* Which reminds me--I am due for a
vacation. What I wouldn't do for a change of scene.

AYDA

Aren't we all.

A moment.

PAVLE

So, when are you due to see Ms. Lagrada again?

Lights fade.

SCENE TEN

The sound of thunder, lightning and rain. We hear the sounds of shoes going up against the stairs.

DRAGA

(in darkness)
My goodness, it's awful out there.

AYDA

(in darkness)
Really coming down...

Then, the rattling of keys. We hear the door open. The light turns on. Enter DRAGA and AYDA, wet. AYDA is closing an umbrella as he enters.

DRAGA

So this is it, then?

AYDA

I'll take your--

AYDA takes her coat and places it on the coat rack.

DRAGA

Thank you.

DRAGA

Oh! It's a little old fashioned, but it is charming.

She crosses to the radio.

DRAGA

I wonder if there's been any developments on the storm.

The sound of the radio adjusting. All of a sudden the lights flicker and turn out. The sound of the power failing.

DRAGA

Oh! It's a little old-fashioned, but charming, nonetheless.

A moment. We hear nothing but their feet moving and the falling rain.

AYDA

Oh, hell.

DRAGA

What do we do now?

AYDA

I've an idea.

DRAGA giggles. We hear them tussling around in the dark for a few moments. Suddenly, the lights rise again. The radio comes to life,

*playing Something Like Lollipop by the Chordettes or Happy Birth-
day, Sweet Sixteen by Neil Sedaka. It gives DRAGA a jump.*

DRAGA

Oh--!

They laugh.

AYDA

Guess the power's back on.

He goes to turn off the radio.

DRAGA

No, keep it on!

AYDA

Keep it on, you say.

*DRAGA extends her hand and inches him closer to her. They dance
closely together. They kiss.*

DRAGA

You want to?

AYDA

Now?

DRAGA

Well, sure. I'm ready for it.

AYDA

You're ready for it.

DRAGA

It's been a while, but it's hardly my first time.

A moment.

DRAGA

It's not yours, is it?

AYDA nods. They laugh nervously. He looks away from her.

DRAGA

That's very sweet. We can pretend it's mine, too.

She begins to unbutton the buttons on his shirt, one by one.

DRAGA

And just like my first time, I'll treat you to some sweets for breakfast tomorrow morning.

AYDA

Okay.

DRAGA

(giggly)
Okay.

The music swells. They kiss. Blackout.

SCENE ELEVEN

The scene has transformed to Meat Packer's Alley, a seedy part of town. If possible, a scrim descends, and visible silhouettes of buildings and meat hooks of flesh dangling from the sky are clearly seen.

In sight is a lamppost which a YOUNG WOMAN leans against. She is wearing sunglasses, a short dress, and a scarf around her head. She is smoking a cigarette and peers out into the distance. In another space A MAN in a dirty apron smokes a human body over an open fire from a trash can, and smoke emerges from the can. At the very edge of the stage is a HOMELESS WOMAN, asleep among a pile of trash. Far downstage is a bench.

Italian opera music plays in the background, along the ambiance of cars passing and honking and people chattering.

After a moment, enter DRAGA and AYDA. Ayda is wearing a new peacock suit jacket and Draga is dressed very fashionably. Him and DRAGA are eating kringlers, wrapped in wax paper.

DRAGA

My father won't go near this place much these days, but really, I can't get enough of it even still.

AYDA

The smell doesn't bother you?

DRAGA

No, not really. Does it bother you?

AYDA

No, in fact, I'm quite used to it. I only asked because for someone who's not used to it, I'd imagine it could make you queasy.

DRAGA

Sometimes, but, it's to be expected. Aren't these pastries just to die for?

AYDA

Heavenly, indeed.

DRAGA

And at one for two shillings. It will hardly surprise you to hear me say this, but, my father's known the owner of that shop for quite some time. His name is Yaakov, and he has a marvelous laugh. He's really a great fellow.

Enter BALABAN.

AYDA

Oh, look! Balaban!

BALABAN

Oh, hello, dear boy!

AYDA

Please let me introduce you. This is Draga Lagrada. Draga, this is my neighbor, Mr. Balaban.

DRAGA

It is good to meet you, sir.

BALABAN

And what brings you two here?

AYDA

We were just strolling around. We just came from getting pastries.

BALABAN

Ah, breakfast! I knew I was missing something. Thanks, Ayda. Miss Lagrada, it was a pleasure meeting you, my dear. I must be off, I just remembered something...what was it again?

DRAGA

Well, we won't keep you, sir. It was nice meeting you too.

BALABAN

Of course, I remembered, they're paying out pensions today! Much obliged, young lady. Now I really must have to go. And Ayda, that jacket--I had no idea you got so rich overnight, congrats.

AYDA

I'll see you around, Balaban.

BALABAN

Good day to the two of you as well.

He exits. At some point, the two sit on the bench.

DRAGA

What a strange man.

AYDA

He's harmless, really.

DRAGA

What was his name?

AYDA

Balaban. I've known him my whole life. He knew my parents too.

DRAGA

Oh.

AYDA

He's like a father to me, in most respects.

DRAGA

Can I ask you something that I hope you won't take offense to?

AYDA

Go ahead.

DRAGA

Do you...*(beat)* Rather, I should say...*(beat)* I'm having trouble finding the words. Darling, what I'm trying to ask is besides myself, Pavle Pechuli and Mr. Balaban, who do you spend time with outside of work?

AYDA

Really just you three, I suppose.

DRAGA

What I admire about you so deeply is that you're mature beyond your years, so intellectual and cerebral, and I can see how that could make someone a bit of a lone wolf—

AYDA

A lone wolf?

DRAGA

Oh, it's an expression from the old days. I never saw a wolf when they were around, but wolves were kind of like a cross between foxes and dogs as I understand it. Grayish, pointed ears, snouts--that sort of thing. Wolves used to travel in packs, but sometimes individual wolves were excluded from their pack for reasons that I suppose only animal psychologists could've really understood, and roamed the earth alone. The phenomenon coined the term "lone wolf". I suppose what I meant was that you keep to yourself--and again, there's nothing wrong with it at all--but I do wonder if you ever have considered expanding your social circles.

AYDA

I don't know. I hadn't thought much of it.

DRAGA

The truth is, I'm out and about constantly, but outside of yourself and a handful of others, there aren't many people I can say are true friends. Which leads me to ask you if you'd join me and come to my father's birthday party in two weeks time--this party is actually the whole reason I bought that peacock when we first met. It's supposed to be a big event with a lot of important people, and I know you don't care much about that kind of a thing, but...

A moment.

DRAGA

It's perfectly fine to say no.

AYDA

Well, um. I--

DRAGA

Really, there's no pressure.

AYDA

I need to think about it. The truth be told is that I'm a bit... worn out at the moment, is all.

DRAGA

I suppose you would be after last night and this morning.

A moment.

DRAGA

Oh, you're blushing! I didn't mean to embarrass you. Oh, aren't you just--?

AYDA

It's not that I'm not enjoying my time with you--

DRAGA

Nonsense. No offense taken. There's no rush, really. *(a long pause)* I hope you'll meet my father when you feel you're up for it. I care about you a great deal and--it's been so long since I've spent this much time with someone and I'm beginning to think I...

A moment. They stare into each other's eyes.

DRAGA

Let's go and call you a cab home, shall we?

Blackout.

SCENE TWELVE

Back at Ayda's apartment. AYDA and BALABAN are having drinks at the island. At rise, AYDA is opening the window to the apartment.

AYDA

That better?

BALABAN

Thank the lord, it's sweltering here. So tell me more about her--has she an education?

AYDA

No, no formal education.

BALABAN

How did the two of you manage to match up?

AYDA

I suppose we managed when the match was made.

BALABAN

Oh, you are so coy!

AYDA

We met at Pavle Pechuli's shop downtown, Pechuli's Den. Pavle is a recent friend of mine.

BALABAN

Oh is he the man you told me about--the jumper who you tried to eat, but it turned out he was still alive?

AYDA

Yes.

BALABAN

Ah. Well, anyway, I didn't mean to pry or assume--

AYDA

You needn't concern yourself. We simply met, that's all, and neither she nor I took it for granted.

BALABAN

How do you mean, for granted? Do you mean it was love at first sight?

AYDA

I suppose.

BALABAN

There is no supposing about it! Well?

Suddenly from offstage, we hear two men yelling:

MAN 1 (O.S)

It's only common sense that if we drive cars on the right side
of the road, we should walk on the right side of the pavement!

MAN 2 (O.S)

Bull! You know very well that what you're suggesting makes
no sense at all--! Or do you have such a high opinion of yourself that you perceive an engine laboring in your ass?!

MAN 1 (O.S)

You wouldn't know an Engine from your own right hand,
you oaf!

MAN 2 (O.S)

And you are suddenly an expert on sidewalks?

BALABAN

(calling)
Gentlemen! Enough!

MAN 1 (O.S)
Oh, shut up, old man!

BALABAN

Go home! It's nearly curfew, you imbeciles!

BALABAN shuts the window.

BALABAN

I couldn't handle living so close to the street like that. I don't know how you do it.

AYDA

The same way you live in that icebox of an apartment! It's like a tundra in the winter.

BALABAN

Bah.

A moment. He takes a drink.

BALABAN

I suppose now that you and Mrs. Lagrada are beginning to get serious, you'll want to leave this place and shack up in her mansion and leave me to rot here.

AYDA

Don't say that, I would never do that.

BALABAN

No, no. I understand. She is your girlfriend now, it's only natural.

AYDA

I don't fully know if she's my girlfriend. I really like her, but it's--like I was saying, we're not at that stage yet. At least, I don't think.

BALABAN

Then what are you? A woman of her age and means isn't just some fling.

A moment.

AYDA

I...care for her. I care for her deeply.

BALABAN

Be that as it may now, you'll fly the coop sooner rather than later. An old man has the ability to sense when the good days are ending.

AYDA

Balaban, in all the years I've known you, I've never known exactly--why didn't you ever get married to the woman you had your daughter with?

BALABAN

Trust me, we were a terrible match. No, not at all right for each other.

AYDA

But surely, there must've been someone else after her, right?
Did you ever come close?

BALABAN

Once or twice, I had a few partners but the uh...how should
I say. The timing wasn't right I suppose. *(beat)* When all's said
and done, I enjoy my own company.

A moment.

BALABAN

Ayda, I'm only going to ask you this once. Is there...*(beat)*
Do you...? *(beat)* Could you foresee a possibility in which you
could talk Draga's father into making an exception for me?
And give me just even one more year?

A silence.

BALABAN

I'm not ready yet. I'm...I'm scared. I'm very scared.

BALABAN embraces AYDA. It lasts a moment.

BALABAN

I'm sorry--I've--I've had too much to drink.

AYDA

No--

BALABAN

Really, I..I shouldn't have said anything. I should go lie down.

AYDA

You don't have to go.

BALABAN

No really, it's almost past my bedtime.

He gets up to exit.

BALABAN

I want you to know that I'm very happy for you and Draga. Joy is in short supply these days, you take it where you can get it. *(beat)* If you need me, you know where to find me.

He exits. A moment. AYDA finishes his wine, turns on the radio. Static. Then, the end of "Etudes" by Chopin plays--only the last few seconds, then--

RADIO HOST

And that was Chopin's Etudes, here at WN99. And now a word from our sponsors--

COMMERCIAL VOICE:

Have you got a case of blues? Are you experiencing a real bummer summer? Well, we've got just what the doctor ordered: an affordable, relaxing and extraordinary getaway. Come on over to Untitled Island C758, just 300 miles away from *(static)* -- perfect for families, couples, and all the lone wolves out there! Come on down! No permission from *(static)* for stays of seven days or less! Experience the beach, the mountains, and a cosy resort all for an exclusive week long getaway package of 500 shillings,
airfare included!

AYDA

Only 500 shillings?

He grabs a napkin and a pen.

COMMERCIAL VOICE

Come on down! Untitled Island C758! Offer only valid for the next 24 hours. Call now- 866-TRAVEL.

He scrambles to write down the number.

COMMERCIAL VOICE

That's 866-Travel. Certain restrictions may apply. Only offer to *(static)* residents only...

Static. Then, a new song plays. AYDA crosses to his couch and reaches deep inside of it and reveals a small box. He opens it and a bunch of shillings spill onto the floor. While the music plays, AYDA counts the coins. He then puts it back into the container. He crosses to the phone and dials. The sound of ringing. Then:

AYDA

Hello, is this 866-Travel? *(beat)* Yes, I'm interested in the getaway package? *(beat)* Yes--is it really only 500 shillings, airfare included?

SCENE THIRTEEN

Back at the morgue. ZAKORA at the slab with a hacksaw.

ZAKORA

Krot!

No response.

ZAKORA

Krot!

KROT enters on, hurriedly.

KROT

Sorry I'm late, chief. You know it was the weekend and you know, I--

ZAKORA

Another sleepless night, eh?

KROT

I was throbbing again, Chief, and well...you know--she's quite an insatiable girl.

KROT crosses to get a hacksaw off of the wall. They begin cutting up the body.

ZAKORA

You truly are a prickled pickled pucker, Krot.

KROT

Well Chief--

ZAKORA

Never mind. In any event, we need to work a bit of overtime this week. Ayda's called out for the week.

KROT

The whole week?

ZAKORA

Yes, and quite frankly, it's about time he got out of here. Look at the guy, he's got a darkness behind his eyes. He's miserable. In the past few years he's worked for me, the man's never taken a day off. He told me he got a deal on the radio for a holiday. I think it'll be good for him.

KROT

Lucky bastard. I want to go on holiday.

ZAKORA

We can see about that once you prove to me you can get to work on time. That reminds me--I got a call late last night that our delivery time has been changed and it's going to start coming earlier from now on. What time is it?

KROT checks the clock on the wall.

KROT

Ten past eight.

ZAKORA

Dammit! They said they were going to come at around to ten to fifteen minutes past, god dammit, Krot!

KROT

Why did they change up the route?

ZAKORA

I don't know! Just go and start getting last night's bins ready.

KROT begins to exit.

ZAKORA

Oh by rigor mortis, boy! Faster!

A moment. The phone rings. ZAKORA goes to answer it.

ZAKORA

Hello? *(beat)* Yes? *(beat)* Uh-huh. Oh. Uh-oh. Well, you know, I'm actually--if you can believe it or not--a man short today.

(beat) Yes, I know it's unusual but--I'm afraid there's--*(beat)* Uh-huh. Ok. I understand. Ok. I will do that. All through the night if we have to. Yes, I. Ok. Yes. Ok. Goodbye.

KROT re-enters with a few labeled bins.

KROT

So I didn't even tell you the best part about last night--

ZAKORA

Krot, you fickled fucker, shut your mouth! The plant's demanding that we have twice the amount of meat ready to ship out than usual by tomorrow morning.

KROT

What? Why?

ZAKORA

Because...I don't know! I'm going to need us to work through the night. You can phone home at lunch.

A knock at the door.

KROT, ZAKORA

I'll get it--

They both go to the door. Enter a DELIVERY MAN, wearing the same delivery uniform as Irina.

DELIVERY MAN

Hello.

A moment.

KROT

Who the hell are you?

DELIVERY MAN

Oh yes--I've heard that quite a lot today. From what I understand, the woman before me left the packaging plant. Anyway, I'll be your Delivery Man from here on out. Do you have those fourteen shipments ready?

ZAKORA throws his hands up in the air and screams. Blackout.

SCENE FOURTEEN

The scene transitions to AYDA going through airport security with a suitcase. Elevator music plays. He is still wearing the peacock jacket. A uniformed AIRPORT SECURITY GUARD gestures for him to raise his arms and she scans him with a handheld metal detector. She scans the suitcase. She gestures for him to pass.

He takes the suitcase and crosses to take his seat on the airplane. The design of the chair is reminiscent of a Pan Am plane from the 1980's, with a loud, vibrant pattern. He takes a postcard from one of his breast pockets and begins writing on it.

Enter BALABAN, reading the postcard.

BALABAN

Dearest Balaban, I apologize for not calling sooner. I simply got too busy. After our conversation last night, I heard an advert on the radio for a getaway package for a week on Untitled Island C758 that boarded this morning. It's now occurring to me that I forgot to forward my mail--would you mind bringing it in? See you in about a week's time.
Best, Ayda.

Enter a FLIGHT ATTENDANT, carrying a cart.

FLIGHT ATTENDANT

Can I get you anything? Coffee? Libation?

AYDA

Libation, please. Do you make Vieux-Carres?

FLIGHT ATTENDANT

We do but I should let you know that all drinks are ten shillings, but shots of brandy are complementary.

AYDA

I'll take a shot of brandy then.

She pours a shot of brandy and hands it to him. He takes the shot.

FLIGHT ATTENDANT

Would you like another? You look like you want another.

AYDA

Sure.

She pours him another shot.

FLIGHT ATTENDANT

Anything else?

AYDA

What else is free?

FLIGHT ATTENDANT

The only other item that's complimentary are our lollies.

AYDA

I'll take a lolly.

She produces a cherry lollipop for him and exits. He unwraps the lollipop and sucks on it. He begins producing another letter. At a certain point, he crunches it and tosses it in the aisle.
Enter PAVLE, reading the postcard.

PAVLE

Dear Pavle, how are you, friend? I'm writing to let you know I've decided to take a holiday at the last minute after I heard an advert on the radio. It's going to be beautiful, I'll try and draw it from memory the best I can when I come back. I wish there was a way of knowing what it looked like before I went, but I know it's going to be special. Anyway, I return on Sunday at 6 am. Could you pick me up at the airport? I can try and phone you when I get to the island and discuss more details. Ciao, Ayda.

AYDA writes another postcard. Enter DRAGA, reading the postcard.

DRAGA

My Dear Draga, I apologize I haven't called today to tell you the big news--I'm going on holiday. Just for a week though.

My first holiday! I'm going to meet new people, just like you suggested to me. I'm sorry I didn't tell you earlier, but the radio advert for the luxury package said I could only claim it if I went now, and so I took some money I'd been saving and went for it. I simply didn't have time to phone anyone besides my boss. It all happened so quickly. Lastly, I wanted to say that after thinking about it, I would be honoured to come to your father's birthday party on Sunday when I get back. I'm excited to meet him. Lo...no, wait...Sinc...no...
Faithfully Yours, Ayda.

Reality begins bending. Lights down on AYDA and shifts towards his everyday life going on without him, without speaking. Something vaguely psychedelic like Tame Impala or The Flaming Lips might play. The ensemble roams the streets and we begin to see a few small moments happen:

PAVLE and DRAGA in Pavle's shop, and WOMAN #1 comes in and buys a taxidermied rooster and some salt from PAVLE.

Letters fall from the sky, and BALABAN catches them.

ZAKORA putting body parts into many, many bins and stacking them. He may stop to smoke a cigarette, out of exhaustion.

A bright light flashes, and everyone freezes, then a hard blackout.

SCENE FIFTEEN

Fog rolls in. We hear the ambiance of a swamp. A sign appears: MEDIUM, 10 SHL. AYDA enters, holding his suitcase. He knocks on the sign.

A VOICE
Come in.

Lights reveal a MEDIUM, with a crystal ball on the table. There is an open seat for AYDA.

AYDA
Hello.

MEDIUM
Hello. Sit.

He does.

AYDA
Do you have a telephone I could borrow?

MEDIUM
You can only use the phone if you pay for a reading.

AYDA

How much?

MEDIUM

Ten shillings. It says so right there on the sign.

AYDA sighs, and gives him ten shillings.

MEDIUM

A bit of a farther walk from the hotel then you thought, hmm?

AYDA

I'd say so.

MEDIUM

I hate to tell you, but it's another three miles by foot. The getaway brochure is a little misleading. It's really not very walkable to the resort. You can call a taxi if you wish, but ten shillings is the rate—take it or leave it.

AYDA

Oh. Ok.

MEDIUM

As for the reading, you can ask me anything you'd like, and I will look into my ball and give you as best an answer I can.

AYDA

What's my name?

MEDIUM

Does it begin with a D?

AYDA

A 'D'?

MEDIUM

Yes. Does your name begin with a D?

AYDA

No.

MEDIUM

Hmm. I'm not seeing it my dear boy. Do you mind telling it to me?

AYDA

Ayda.

MEDIUM

Thank you, Ayda. And Ayda, what is it you would like to learn about yourself from a reading today?

AYDA

I don't really want to know anything in particular. I don't really want to have a reading either, if I'm being perfectly honest.

MEDIUM

And could that be because you're guarded, you keep to yourself a lot and don't really let others in?

A moment.

AYDA

I guess that's not inaccurate.

MEDIUM

You live alone and let me see what else the ball is telling me... *(stares into the ball)* You work for... *(beat)* Well I can't quite see, but you don't work around many people, do you?

AYDA

Not many, no.

MEDIUM

And you're lonely, yes? You're looking for someone to share your life with, but you're not sure, who this person might be, right?

A moment. AYDA considers.

AYDA

Well, not necessarily.

MEDIUM

Ah, that's right. You have a lover, but you're not satisfied
with all of her.

AYDA

What is her name?

MEDIUM

Whose?

AYDA

My lover's name. If I have a lover, what is her name?

MEDIUM

The crystal ball seldomly shows names, it...it shows me pictures and images...

AYDA

What does she look like then?

MEDIUM

Oh, yes...she...she's young. Beautiful. Tall, thin. Brown hair.

AYDA

Okay. And what is she like? What does her home look like?

MEDIUM

Oh she's poor, very lonely too. She is longing to marry you and make a family together.

AYDA

Do you see us getting married, then.

MEDIUM

It's going to be on the rooftop of a building. A city wedding. Very modern and urban.

AYDA

Do you see us having children?

MEDIUM

Yes--many children. One looks just like you, one that looks more like her, and the youngest, that looks like a little bit of both of you.

AYDA

Lovely. Alright. Well then, I suppose now is a good time to tell you that my girlfriend is not tall, thin, young, or has brown hair. Nor is she lonely and she is especially not poor. In fact, quite the opposite. She is also not of child bearing age at all. I care for her nonetheless, but needless to say, this reading is completely bogus and I would really like to use your phone now.

MEDIUM

I'm sorry, Alan.

AYDA

Ayda.

MEDIUM

Ayda--right, yes. I'm sorry, the gift didn't come as easily with you. Some people are so secretive and skeptical, that they don't want themselves to be seen in the ball.

AYDA opens his wallet and gives him ten shillings.

AYDA

May I make my call now and fetch a cab?

MEDIUM

Straight on through the back.

AYDA

Thank you.

He exits. Blackout.

SCENE SIXTEEN

The dock transforms and faces the audience. The sound of waves crashing. The lights take the form of water reflecting off the surface--shimmery and in ripples.

If possible, an image of a brightly colored polluted ocean is projected behind the dock.

On the dock is WOMAN #1, wearing sunglasses and a one-piece holding a tanning reflector to her face, sitting on a beach chair.

Something like "Blue Christmas" by Elvis Presley plays in the background.

After a moment, AYDA enters in an old-fashioned striped swimming romper, goggles, and a swim cap.

AYDA
(*disgusted*)
Oh, god.

He is beyond disappointed. He takes off his goggles and turns to the WOMAN.

AYDA
Can you believe this?!

WOMAN #1

Hmm?

AYDA

This water--it's filled with cans, and bottles and all sorts of rubbish! The lodge said this was the best spot in town.

WOMAN #1

It is, compared to the other beaches. *(beat)* Still not much good for swimming, though.

She briefly sets down her tanning shield, and picks up a pineapple cup sitting next to her. It is important that it is an actual pineapple.

AYDA

What've you got there?

WOMAN #1

Just a splash of vodka and club soda. In a pineapple. Would you fancy that?

AYDA

A pineapple? What on earth?

WOMAN #1

It's a fruit. I know, there's not any of these back at home. You can eat it, too. Ask for one at the inn. They'll give you some vodka and club soda in it for five shillings. Now, if you'll excuse me, I want to close my eyes for a bit.

She sets her drink down and picks up the reflector again. AYDA looks on in disbelief, and sighs. A moment as he listens to the ocean. Eventually, AYDA exits, and the lights turn to blue and focus on WOMAN #1, who begins to fall asleep and snore.

The music becomes more and more distorted, and the lights begin to dim, until it fades to black.

Over the distorted music in the darkness, we hear the sound of snoring a voice of the FLIGHT ATTENDANT:

FLIGHT ATTENDANT (V.O):
Excuse me? *(beat)* Excuse me, sir? *(beat)* Sir?

Lights abruptly rise to AYDA in the seat of the plane from earlier, snoring. Next to him is the FLIGHT ATTENDANT with her cart. She gently startles him awake. Next to him is a suitcase.

AYDA
Hm-huh?

FLIGHT ATTENDANT
Apologies sir, it's just--I hate to embarrass you, but some of the passengers are complaining you're snoring a little too loudly.

AYDA

Oh. I...I'm so sorry.

FLIGHT ATTENDANT

It's quite alright.

AYDA

Could I trouble you for a complimentary shot of brandy, or even a lolly, like the last flight?

FLIGHT ATTENDANT

Unfortunately, we ran out of both while you were asleep. I could offer you a complimentary set of severed human lips, though.

AYDA

I'm ok, thank you. How much longer until we land?

FLIGHT ATTENDANT

Very, very, soon.

She exits. Lights fade on them.

In a separate space, lights rise on PAVLE waving.

PAVLE

Over here! Over here!

AYDA runs over, suitcase in hand.

PAVLE

Good to see you my friend!

AYDA

And you as well.

PAVLE

How was it? Tell me everything! What did it look like?

AYDA

Truth be told friend, it was a bit underwhelming. The oceans
were completely filled with waste and rubbish. You couldn't
swim at all. But I got some much needed rest, so that was
nice.

PAVLE

What was the food like? Surely there weren't any jumpers.

AYDA

Unfortunately I had to make do. I didn't eat much though.
The seasoning they use for their meat is much more vibrant
though, I will give them that. They also had some clone of a
fruit called a pineapple there! I didn't even know there were
other cloned fruit besides lemons and pears.

PAVLE

Ah yes, I've read about pineapples. What about the women,
though? How were they?

AYDA

Oh, I avoided them. I'm a spoken for man now, no use for a
wandering eye.

PAVLE

So you and Ms. Lagrada are official, then?

AYDA

Official enough, I'm afraid. I'm going to meet her father
tonight. It's his grand birthday party.

PAVLE

A big step...!

A moment.

PAVLE

How do you feel about meeting him?

AYDA

I feel...I feel, um...*(he tries to find the words)* I feel like a traitor.
He stands against everything I believe in. I had a lot of time
to think to myself and think things over, and I've thought

quite a bit about the importance of authenticity. Before my father died, he always told me to be an honest man no matter what, and ever since I've been with Draga, I've been skirting my real feelings. In a few days time, once this birthday celebration is over, I will come clean to her about my true feelings about her father, the Ethics Committee, and maybe even the jumpers. I can't keep building a relationship founded on lies.

PAVLE

And then what?

AYDA

I'm not quite sure. Pray that she takes it well, I suppose.

A moment. PAVLE reassuringly pats him on the back.

PAVLE

You'll do the right thing, I know it. And if it doesn't work out, it wasn't meant to be.

Blackout.

SCENE SEVENTEEN

In a similar set up to Meatpacker's Alley, the scrim descends, and we see the shadows of the entire ensemble, casting against the theatre. We hear a crowd laughing and drinking. Then, the repeated clinking of a glass as to call attention. A faint shadow of a larger man speaking, and holding a misshapen object comes into view.

COSIMO

Attention, attention. *(beat)* Tonight we have things fresh--the freshest of foods, all of which will in your guts mesh: loins of an old lady; athlete pâté; neighbors' cuts; a bit of a lawyer's stiff neck; supple breasts from those who never rest, who dance the night away, accepting every advance; cured killer's lips; muscled thighs and soup hips; schoolboys ribs; shy liver of a gorge giver; groin with no balls of a cop on call; shingles of a priest in a stew you want to eat; tongue of a writer, you'll lick the plate, buttocks fat and great; giblets of a politician to steady your nerves before voting as he deserves; the less we speak of the intestines the better – though the sausages are delicious; something ground of a CEO, this one was quite the fatty, better you should eat him then to have his meat pecked by a murder of crows, on the spikes around town; lean kebabs in various sums; the dentists toothless gums; new from the banker, rich with no fat to embellish, meat of his shoulders for your interest-less relish, so that you live to see better days, some more sausages from the boss who pays you; from a salesman, door to door, or on the other end of a phone, and on sale, rosy thighs from an A Level schoolgirl for you to crave; pick-led wrists of a monopolist. It's not a nifty rhyme, I know, that's how it is when hunger's for show. Whatever your heart desires, our meat is your meat to hire and I hope you take it all in--for you are all looking fine and splendid, and we are in the best of company tonight, and I cannot thank my daughter or the Ethics Committee enough for this fabulous soiree and for all these wonderful rare and exotic gifts they have bestowed to me. I could not think of a better way to celebrate my 70th birthday. Cheers, to all of us.

Everyone raises their glasses.

ALL

To all of us!

Everyone claps. We hear everyone carrying on in the background, and slowly throughout the following scene, the shadows fade into darkness. Then, three figures emerge out of the shadows: AYDA in his classic peacock jacket, COSIMO and DRAGA. COSIMO is carrying the peacock in his arms.

COSIMO

It is so great to finally meet you after all this time. My Draga almost sings when she speaks of you.

AYDA

That's...sweet of her.

DRAGA

I never say anything that isn't true.

COSIMO

Ayda, a word? Between two gentlemen.

DRAGA

Fine, but not for too long!

COSIMO

Run along love, we'll catch up with you shortly. Oh, and would you mind putting the peacock in back, darling?

DRAGA takes the peacock and kisses him on the cheek and exits. The rest of the ENSEMBLE fades away. The TWO cross downstage.

COSIMO

So, Ayda. It is perhaps no secret that Draga has not brought home a man in quite some time. They all seem to...drop off after the first or second date.

AYDA

Oh, well...uh...

COSIMO

And you are a great deal younger than she. A solid twenty years I'd guess? Is that right?

AYDA

I, well, yes--

COSIMO

No matter. Allow me to make you an offer. Right here, right now. If you wed my daughter, I will pay for a new house for both of you and I can give you a spot on the Ethics Board.

A silence.

AYDA

I...I don't know what to say.

COSIMO

Say nothing. Just listen to me, son. I just want her to be happy. To be frank, she's blown through my money, and now is burning a rather large hole in my pocket. The poor girl just isn't cut out to work. See, she's enamored with you—she is absolutely obsessed. But let's be honest, she's running out of time. In fact, she's been out of time. And I don't know your situation really—I mean, she constantly tells me how smart and poetic you are, and why should I not believe her? I can give you a new job that pays a very handsome salary a year, with paid time off, benefits—vacation perks, even. *(Beat, a whisper:)* You know, there are places—uncharted islands— where board members can go where there are real plants and animals--not clones--but the real thing, that you can eat.

Beautiful creatures--peacocks, kangaroos, elephants run wild. All different fruits too--I could go on. The point is, there are things on those islands you've never seen in your life.

AYDA

I've just been to Untitled Island C758 for the first time, and--

COSIMO

These islands are better, much better than that place. Oh, god. You'll make me laugh. You have no idea. They're indescribable really. They're life-changing.

A moment.

AYDA

But the Ethics Committee...is in charge of...executing people.

COSIMO

That is, one part of the job, yes. And it's not easy, and it's not for everyone. But it is better to handle the strings then be the puppet, no?

AYDA

I don't follow.

COSIMO

It is better to be behind the table making the decisions, then in front of the table, begging for mercy.

A silence.

COSIMO

How about this? Let me show you something that may change your mind. Here's what the salary for an Ethics Board member is.

COSIMO takes out a notecard from a coat pocket and a pen. COSIMO writes it down, and gives the notecard to AYDA. AYDA's eyes widen.

COSIMO

Think about it. This could be the beginning of a whole new life for you.

A WOMAN'S VOICE

Oh, Cosimo! I need you this instant to tell Miriam that hysterical joke you told last Thursday at the country club!

COSIMO

I'm being summoned. Catch up with you soon?

COSIMO pats AYDA on the shoulder and exits. AYDA's eyes are transfixed on the card.

A tight spotlight surrounds him. He then looks to us with an incredulous expression.

Something like "Both Sides Now" covered by Neil Diamond plays.

END OF PLAY.

INSIDE

Sean Pollock is a multidisciplinary writer, director, designer, and teaching artist. Select directing/playwriting credits include: *The Bed Show* (Philly Theatre Week), *This Is A Play About Newscasters* (Prop Thtr, Chicago), *Up In Flames* (Rising Sun Governor's Island Residency), *The Weird* (The Brick, NYC), *American Juggalo* (HERE Arts Center, NYC) and *A Very Merry Unauthorized Children's Scientology Pageant* (54 Below and Greenroom 42, NYC). Touring: *I'm Smiling Because I'm Uncomfortable* (NYC, Maine, Dickinson College, San Diego Fringe. Winner: Best Site Specific Performance, San Diego Fringe). Off-Broadway: *Trump Rally* (Theatre Row). He has contributed to the Onstage Blog, Thought Catalog, and zines such as Loose Tooth, Notes, and Circus Of Dreams. He has taught at Theatre Horizon, 82nd St Academics, Wingspan Arts and in the public school district of Philadelphia. Currently, his play based on urban folklore and true crime stories from his home state of New Jersey, entitled *Land Of The Free, Home Of The Weird*, is being commissioned by American Lore Theatre for whenever we can do live theatre again. He is also developing several short animated films. In his spare time, he can be found collaging, taking pictures on disposable cameras, and phonebanking for progressive candidates. Training: Ithaca College, NTI, Directors Lab North, Directors Lab Chicago, Directors Lab West. Dramatists Guild Member. www.seanpollock.net, insta: @seanp_yo.